La Belle Dame Sans Merci
Shmoop Poetry Guide

About this Learning Guide

Shmoop Will Make You a Better Lover*
*of Literature, History, Poetry, Life...

Our lively learning guides are written by experts and educators who want to show your brain a good time. Shmoop writers come primarily from Ph.D. programs at top universities, including Stanford, Harvard, and UC Berkeley.

Want more Shmoop? We cover literature, poetry, bestsellers, music, US history, civics, biographies (and the list keeps growing). Drop by our website to see the latest.

www.shmoop.com

©2010 Shmoop University, Inc. All Rights Reserved.
Talk to the Labradoodle... She's in Charge.

La Belle Dame Sans Merci
Shmoop Poetry Guide

Table of Contents

Introduction . . . 3
   In a Nutshell . . . 3
   Why Should I Care? . . . 3

The Poem . . . 4

Overview and Line-by-Line Summary . . . 5
   Brief Summary . . . 5
   Stanzas 1 & 2 . . . 5
   Stanzas 3 & 4 . . . 6
   Stanzas 5 & 6 . . . 7
   Stanzas 7 & 8 . . . 8
   Stanzas 9 & 10 . . . 9
   Stanzas 11 & 12 . . . 9

Technique . . . 10
   Symbols, Imagery, & Wordplay . . . 10
   Form and Meter . . . 13
   Speaker . . . 14
   Sound Check . . . 14
   What's Up With the Title? . . . 15
   Calling Card . . . 15
   Tough-O-Meter . . . 15
   Setting . . . 15

Themes . . . 16
   Theme of Love . . . 16
   Questions About Love . . . 16
   Chew on this: Love . . . 16
   Theme of Women and Femininity . . . 16
   Questions About Women and Femininity . . . 17
   Chew on this: Women and Femininity . . . 17
   Theme of The Supernatural . . . 17
   Questions About The Supernatural . . . 17
   Chew on this: The Supernatural . . . 17
   Theme of Versions of Reality . . . 18
   Questions About Versions of Reality . . . 18
   Chew on this: Versions of Reality . . . 18
   Theme of Abandonment . . . 18
   Questions About Abandonment . . . 18
   Chew on this: Abandonment . . . 19

Quotes . . . 19
   Love Quotes . . . 19
   Women and Femininity Quotes . . . 20
   The Supernatural Quotes . . . 21
   Versions of Reality Quotes . . . 22
   Abandonment Quotes . . . 23

La Belle Dame Sans Merci
Shmoop Poetry Guide

Study Questions	24
Did You Know?	24
Trivia	24
Steaminess Rating	24
Allusions and Cultural References	25
Best of the Web	25
Websites	25
Video	25
Audio	26
Images	26
Historical Documents	26
Books	27
Movies and TV	27
Shmoop's Poetry Primer	27
How to Read Poem	27
What is Poetry?	29
Poetry Glossary	31

La Belle Dame Sans Merci
Shmoop Poetry Guide

Introduction

In a Nutshell

John Keats was an English poet writing in the early 19th century, towards the end of what became known as the "Romantic period." The Romantic period isn't just about love stories – it was a political and social movement as well as a literary one. The Romantics were reacting to an 18th century obsession with order, rationality, and scientific precision. Romantic writers felt that these Enlightenment-era thinkers missed the point about what it meant to be human. After all, they argued, you can't write an equation to define human nature. So the Romantic movement was partly a backlash against the rationalism of the 18th century Enlightenment.

When critics talk about the Romantic poets, they usually focus on the "big six": William Blake, William Wordsworth, and Samuel Taylor Coleridge were the oldest of the six, and the younger generation included Percy Bysshe Shelley, Lord Byron, and our man, John Keats. Keats was the youngest of the six, but he was, alas, the first to die. He was only 25 years old when he died of tuberculosis in February 1821. Who knows what might have happened if he'd lived longer?

When Keats found out that he'd caught tuberculosis from nursing his brother, Tom, he was in despair (a diagnosis of tuberculosis in those days was like a death sentence). Keats felt that he'd just made a breakthrough in his writing, and was only beginning to write the kind of poetry that he was really capable of writing. Keats died in Italy, where the doctors thought the warmer weather might extend his life. He asked that his grave bear only the words "Here lies one whose name was writ in water," because he didn't think that he'd lived up to his potential – his life was too short to be memorable, and his poetry was like words "written in water." Boy, was he wrong – he's now celebrated as one of the most famous English poets of all time, despite his premature death.

"La Belle Dame Sans Merci" was written towards the end of his life, after his brother Tom died, but before he found out that he was dying of the same disease. Keats wrote it in 1819, but it wasn't published until 1820. The version that was published includes a lot of changes recommended by his friend and fellow poet, Leigh Hunt. Most critics, though, prefer the original version, so that's what we use in this guide. You'll know the difference right off the bat: the original version begins with the line, "O what can ail thee, knight at arms," while the edited 1820 version opens with, "Ah, what can ail thee, wretched wight."

Why Should I Care?

"La Belle Dame Sans Merci" seems, on the surface, to be just another Romantic poem about knights who fall in love with beautiful (in this case, fairy or elfish) ladies. But wait: in this poem, the guy in question is literally on the verge of death because of his romantic encounter with this woman. What's the deal with that? She didn't stab him or anything – the poem isn't explicit about why the knight is dying. It's left partly to our imagination.

So what kills the knight? He becomes so enraptured with this pretty fairy lady that he forgets everything else. Her kisses put him into a coma, and that's how the speaker of the poem finds him. Ultimately, this poem is about the dangers of obsession, in general: drug addiction,

La Belle Dame Sans Merci
Shmoop Poetry Guide

romantic or erotic obsession, you name it. Keats seems to suggest that the fate of his "knight at arms" could happen to any of us, at any time. So whenever you're tempted to neglect your responsibilities in order to feed an obsession, you should think about what happened to the "knight at arms" in Keats's poem.

The Poem

"O WHAT can ail thee, knight-at-arms,
Alone and palely loitering?
The sedge has wither'd from the lake,
And no birds sing.

"O what can ail thee, knight-at-arms!
So haggard and so woe-begone?
The squirrel's granary is full,
And the harvest's done.

"I see a lily on thy brow
With anguish moist and fever-dew.
And on thy cheeks a fading rose
Fast withereth too."

"I met a lady in the meads,
Full beautiful – a faery's child,
Her hair was long, her foot was light,
And her eyes were wild.

"I made a garland for her head,
And bracelets too, and fragrant zone;
She look'd at me as she did love,
And made sweet moan.

"I set her on my pacing steed,
And nothing else saw all day long;
For sidelong would she bend, and sing
A faery's song.

"She found me roots of relish sweet,
And honey wild and manna-dew;
And sure in language strange she said,
'I love thee true.'

"She took me to her elfin grot,

La Belle Dame Sans Merci
Shmoop Poetry Guide

And there she wept and sigh'd full sore;
And there I shut her wild, wild eyes
With kisses four.

"And there she lullèd me asleep,
And there I dream'd – ah! woe betide!
The latest dream I ever dream'd
On the cold hill's side.

"I saw pale kings and princes too,
Pale warriors, death-pale were they all:
They cried, 'La belle Dame sans Merci
Hath thee in thrall!'

"I saw their starved lips in the gloam
With horrid warning gapèd wide,
And I awoke and found me here
On the cold hill's side.

"And this is why I sojourn here
Alone and palely loitering,
Though the sedge is wither'd from the lake,
And no birds sing."

Overview and Line-by-Line Summary

Brief Summary

The speaker of the poem comes across a "knight at arms" alone, and apparently dying, in a field somewhere. He asks him what's going on, and the knight's answer takes up the rest of the poem. The knight says that he met a beautiful fairy lady in the fields. He started hanging out with her, making flower garlands for her, letting her ride on his horse, and generally flirting like knights do. Finally, she invited him back to her fairy cave. Sweet, thought the knight. But after they were through smooching, she "lulled" him to sleep, and he had a nightmare about all the knights and kings and princes that the woman had previously seduced – they were all dead. And then he woke up, alone, on the side of a hill somewhere.

Stanzas 1 & 2

Stanza 1, Lines 1-4
"O WHAT can ail thee, knight-at-arms,
Alone and palely loitering?
The sedge has wither'd from the lake,
And no birds sing.

La Belle Dame Sans Merci
Shmoop Poetry Guide

- The poem opens with a question: an unnamed speaker asks a "knight at arms" what's wrong, or what's "ail[ing]" him.
- Something is clearly wrong with the knight – he's "loitering" by himself around the edge of a lake, and he's "pale."
- The speaker says that the "sedge," or marsh plants, have all died out from around the lake, and "no birds sing." So we're guessing that it's autumn or even early winter since all the birds have migrated, and the plants have "withered."
- The presence of the "knight at arms" reminds us of medieval fairy tales with knights and ladies in towers. We think that this is the response Keats intended

Stanza 2, Lines 5-8
"O what can ail thee, knight-at-arms,
So haggard and so woe-begone?
The squirrel's granary is full,
And the harvest's done.

- The first part of the stanza echoes the first line of the poem word-for-word. Apparently the knight doesn't answer immediately, so the unnamed speaker has to repeat the question.
- This time, we get two more adjectives to describe the knight: he's "haggard," or worn-out and tired-looking, and "woe-begone." The knight is obviously both sick and depressed.
- The last two lines of the stanza do more to set the scene: the squirrels have finished filling up their "granary," or storage of food for the winter, and the crops have already been harvested.
- We can now safely assume that it's late autumn.

Stanzas 3 & 4

Stanza 3, Lines 9-12
"I see a lily on thy brow
With anguish moist and fever-dew.
And on thy cheeks a fading rose
Fast withereth too."

- The speaker continues to address this sick, depressed "knight at arms." He asks about the "lily" on the knight's "brow," suggesting that the knight's face is pale like a lily.
- The knight's forehead is sweaty with "anguish" and with "fever," so he's obviously sick.
- The last two lines of the stanza describe how the healthy color is rapidly "fading" from the knight's cheeks.

La Belle Dame Sans Merci
Shmoop Poetry Guide

Stanza 4, Lines 13-16
"I met a lady in the meads,
Full beautiful – a faery's child,
Her hair was long, her foot was light,
And her eyes were wild.

- This stanza changes point of view.
- All of a sudden, the knight answers the unnamed speaker's questions. So now the "I" is the knight, rather than the original speaker.
- The knight says that he met a beautiful, fairy-like "lady" in the "meads," or fields.
- She had long hair, was graceful, and had "wild" eyes. (We're not sure what "wild" eyes would look like, but apparently the knight thought it was attractive.)

Stanzas 5 & 6

Stanza 5, Lines 17-20
"I made a garland for her head,
And bracelets too, and fragrant zone;
She look'd at me as she did love,
And made sweet moan.

- The knight made a flower wreath, or "garland," for the lady, along with flower "bracelets."
- The "fragrant zone" is a belt made of flowers.
- We get the idea that the knight decks out the maiden with flowers.
- "Fragrant zone" could also be a reference to her lady parts, which would make sense, given where the next two lines go.
- And where do the next two lines go? Well, the lady is "look[ing]" at the knight while "lov[ing]" and "moan[ing]," so we think that they two are having sex.

Stanza 6, Lines 21-24
"I set her on my pacing steed,
And nothing else saw all day long;
For sidelong would she bend, and sing
A faery's song.

- The knight puts the lady on his horse (his "pacing steed") to take a ride. Yes, there might be sexy connotations to this line, too.
- The knight is so absorbed with his erotic encounter with this fairy lady that he doesn't notice anything else "all day long."
- The lady leans "sidelong," or sideways off of the horse and sings "fairy songs" to the

La Belle Dame Sans Merci
Shmoop Poetry Guide

knight.

Stanzas 7 & 8

Stanza 7, Lines 25-28
"She found me roots of relish sweet,
And honey wild and manna-dew;
And sure in language strange she said,
'I love thee true.'

- The knight says that the fairy lady found him tasty roots, honey, and manna to eat ("of relish sweet").
- "Manna" is the food that the Jewish scriptures say that the Israelites ate when they were wandering around the desert after Moses freed them from slavery in Egypt. It's supposed to be food from heaven, so this word makes the fairy lady seem supernatural, if not actually divine.
- Alternatively, the association could be with the slavery from which the Israelites had just been freed. After all, the knight does become enslaved to the beautiful fairy lady. This allusion becomes even more potent when it's associated with the "honey wild" that the fairy lady fed the knight. (The Israelites were trying to find the Promised Land, which would flow with "milk and honey.")
- The fairy lady tells the knight that she loves him, but she says it "in language strange."
- He doesn't say what language it is, or how he's able to understand her. Maybe he's just hearing what he wants to hear, or maybe her magical influence has enabled him to understand her "language strange."

Stanza 8, Lines 29-32
"She took me to her elfin grot,
And there she wept and sigh'd full sore;
And there I shut her wild, wild eyes
With kisses four.

- The fairy lady takes the knight to her "elfin grot." "Elfin" just means having to do with elves, as any Tolkien fans probably figured. And a "grot" is a grotto, or cave.
- Once they're back at her fairy cave, she cries and sighs loudly. The knight doesn't say why she's crying, and we never find out – it's left to our imagination.
- The knight kisses her weepy eyes four times. (Why "four" kisses? Isn't "three" usually the magic number in fairy tales?)
- Again, her eyes are described as "wild," and this time it's repeated twice.

La Belle Dame Sans Merci
Shmoop Poetry Guide

Stanzas 9 & 10

Stanza 9, Lines 33-36
*"And there she lullèd me asleep,
And there I dream'd – ah! woe betide!
The latest dream I ever dream'd
On the cold hill's side.*

- The fairy lady "lulls" the knight to sleep like a baby in her cave, and he starts to dream something.
- He interrupts himself with a dash – in line 34, and exclaims "Ah! woe betide!" because even the memory of the dream is horrible as he repeats it to the unnamed speaker.
- "Woe betide!" is an archaic exclamation used to express extreme grief or suffering. It was old-fashioned even when Keats was writing.
- The knight's use of this expression emphasizes the medieval romance setting.
- The knight's dream in the fairy cave is the "latest," or last, dream he'll ever have.

Stanza 10, Lines 37-40
*"I saw pale kings and princes too,
Pale warriors, death-pale were they all:
They cried, 'La belle Dame sans Merci
Hath thee in thrall!'*

- The knight describes the dream he had: he saw "kings," "princes," and "warriors, and they were all "death pale." In fact, he repeats the word "pale" three times in two lines.
- This procession of "pale" men could be an allusion to the fourth horseman of the Apocalypse that gets described in the Book of Revelation in the Christian bible. The fourth horseman is Death, and he rides on a pale horse.
- The pale warriors, princes, and kings all cry out in unison that "La belle dame sans merci" has the knight "in thrall," or in bondage.
- Line 39 has the title of the poem in it, so it's time to translate it. The title is French and it translates to "the beautiful woman without mercy."
- (If you want to know more about the title, go to the "What's Up With the Title?" section, and then come back.)

Stanzas 11 & 12

Stanza 11, Lines 41-44
*"I saw their starved lips in the gloom
With horrid warning gapèd wide*

La Belle Dame Sans Merci
Shmoop Poetry Guide

And I awoke and found me here
On the cold hill's side.

- The knight continues to describe the pale warriors from his dream – in the "gloam," or dusk, all he can make out are their "lips."
- Their mouths are "starv'd" and hungry-looking, and their mouths are all open as they cry out their warning to the knight.
- The word "gloam" just means dusk or twilight, but it's no accident that Keats uses it – after all, "gloam" sounds a lot like "gloom."
- The knight wakes up from the dream alone and cold on the side of a hill.

Stanza 12, Lines 45-48
"And this is why I sojourn here
Alone and palely loitering,
Though the sedge is wither'd from the lake,
And no birds sing."

- The knight has finished his story. He tells the original, unnamed speaker, that this is why he's hanging out ("sojourn[ing]" and "loitering") by himself, even though it's so dismal outside.
- The knight repeats the unnamed speaker's words from the first stanza, so that the poem ends with almost exactly the same stanza with which it began.

Technique

Symbols, Imagery, & Wordplay
Welcome to the land of symbols, imagery, and wordplay. Before you travel any further, please know that there may be some thorny academic terminology ahead. Never fear, Shmoop is here. Check out our "How to Read a Poem" section for a glossary of terms.

DramaticFlowers
"La Belle Dame Sans Merci" is so full of flowers, it could practically open its own sidewalk kiosk. Most of the flower imagery in the poem has some kind of symbolic weight to it. We usually associate flowers with springtime, with love, and with life, but that's not always the case in "La Belle Dame Sans Merci." These flowers can be kind of tricky, but never fear. Shmoop is here to help you untangle some of those ambiguous images.

- Line 9: Lilies are often associated with death in Western culture, so the "lily" on the knight's forehead doesn't bode well for him. We can also be pretty sure that the knight doesn't have a flower glued to his forehead, so the speaker is employing a **metaphor** when he says that he "see[s] a lily on thy brow." Besides the association with death, lilies

La Belle Dame Sans Merci
Shmoop Poetry Guide

- are pale white, so a slightly less morbid reading of this line would be that the knight isn't dying, but is just sickly pale.
- Line 11: Roses are often associated with love in Western culture (hence all the advertisements around Valentine's Day), but the knight's "rose" is "fading" and "wither[ing]." Sounds like a pretty clear **metaphor** for the end of a romantic relationship. But like the lily, the rose describes the knight's complexion. The rose is "fading" from the knight's "cheeks." So the rose **metaphor** is doing double duty – it's describing both his "fading" love affair, and his increasingly pale complexion.
- Lines 17-18: The knight makes a flower "garland" and "bracelets" for the fairy lady. He decks her out in flowers. If the knight associates flowers with love and life the way we usually do, it's pretty clear that he's totally in love (or at least in lust) with her.
- Line 18: A "fragrant zone" is a flower belt – it's another string of flowers that the knight offers the fairy lady. But it could also be a **euphemism** for her anatomical "zone" right underneath the belt.

Seasons and Cycles

The beginning and end of the poem seem to take place during autumn or even early winter, but the sequence with the fairy lady seems to be during spring or summer. Does the fairy lady control the seasons? Or does her beauty make the knight think that winter is summer?

- Lines 3: "Sedge" is a grass-like plant that grows in marshy, wet ground close to lakes. If all the "sedge" is "wither'd," it's probably close to autumn, right? We usually associate images of autumn and fallen leaves with old age and imminent death, so this doesn't bode well for the knight.
- Line 4: Where are all the birds? Have they all migrated south for the winter? Wherever they went, their absence makes the landscape of the poem seem even more desolate than the "wither'd" "sedge."
- Line 7: A "granary" is a barn or warehouse used to store grain. The "squirrel" in this line probably doesn't have a literal building to store its nuts, so "granary" is a **metaphor** for the squirrel's hiding places that **personifies** the squirrel by associating it with characteristics and activities usually reserved for humans.
- Line 8: If all the crops have been harvested, then the fields are all empty and deserted. If the "sedge" is dead, the birds are gone, and all the crops are harvested, does that mean that the knight and the unnamed speaker are the only two living things in the landscape? There's good news about the image, though: "harvest" suggests planting, fertility, and the cycle of life – after all, the farmers who brought in the harvest are going to plant seeds again in the spring, and the cycle will repeat itself next year.

Paleness

Considering that the poem opens with descriptions of autumn and the "wither[ing]" plants around the lake, it's not surprising that the landscape and the people in it are colorless. But it is surprising when you tally up how many times the poet uses the word "pale," or synonyms for it. Why does he harp on the paleness? Let's take a look at some examples...

La Belle Dame Sans Merci
Shmoop Poetry Guide

- Line 2: The unnamed speaker says that the knight is "palely loitering." We get the point that he's hanging out by the lake without an obvious purpose, and he's "pale." Read this line out loud: notice the repeated L sound in "Alone and palely loitering"? The **consonance** of the L sound makes the line sound musical (think, "tra-la-la-la-la-la!"), but it also draws our attention to those words, especially to the unusual use of "palely" as an adverb. The word "palely" also creates an **internal rhyme** with the words "ail thee" from line 1. Associating those words makes it clear that the knight's paleness has to do with whatever it is that is "ail[ing]" him.
- Line 9: We hear more about the paleness of the knight when the unnamed speaker uses a flower **metaphor** to point out the "lily" whiteness of the knight's face.
- Lines 37-8: The knight uses the word "pale" three times in two lines. He's describing the dream he had in the fairy lady's cave, and the "pale kings" and "pale warriors" that he saw. They're all "death pale," so now paleness is being explicitly associated with death.
- Lines 37-40: The repetition of the word "pale" in this stanza brings out the similarity between that word and the words "all," "belle," and "thrall." This **consonance**, or repeated sound, associates those words as we read them, making the reader pause to consider how the "*belle* dame" might be responsible for the "*pale*[ness]" of "*all*" the knights she has had "in *thrall*."

Dreams and Sleep
The entire poem could sound like a dream sequence or a fantasy, with all the fairy ladies and "elfin grots." But there's an explicit dream sequence described by the knight at the close of the poem, which brings up questions about consciousness and the nature of reality, and other things that keep us up at night.

- Line 33: The word "lulled" is such a sleepy-sounding word that it's almost **onomatopoeia**: it sounds like what it's supposed to mean.
- Lines 34-5: The word "dream" gets repeated three times in two lines. This can't be an accident. Is the knight wanting to insist that the vision he saw was, in fact, a dream, and not a real event? Is he insisting too much?
- Line 40: The harsh repetition of the *th* sound in this line is enough to wake anyone up. The **consonance** of "Hath thee in thrall!" is what ends the knight's dream. In the next stanza, he sees their mouths open after having "cried" their "warning," and then he wakes up.

Dew and Water
Medieval romances often associate women with water, so it's no surprise that Keats borrows from that tradition in "La Belle Dame Sans Merci." The problem with women and water, though, is that men who mess around with women end up getting all soggy and wet. According to this symbolic tradition, men are weakened by their contact with women.

- Line 3: Already in this line, the speaker is associating death and "wither[ing]" with a body of water: the "lake." And it's not just any body of water. Lakes, unlike springs or rivers, don't

La Belle Dame Sans Merci
Shmoop Poetry Guide

flow (or at least, don't flow quickly), so the water in them stagnates and can grow nasty algae and pond scum.
- Line 10: The unnamed speaker notices that the knight's face is "moist" with "fever dew." OK, so he's sweating because he has a fever. But where did he catch the fever? Look where that word "dew" is repeated…
- Line 26: The knight says that the fairy lady fed him "manna dew." "Manna" is the heavenly food that the Jewish Scriptures say that the Israelites ate in the wilderness after they escaped from slavery. But why, "dew"? Why is the manna in liquid form? It seems likely that the answer is connected with the rest of the complicated system of **metaphor** around water and dew in this poem.

Form and Meter

Ballad, Iambic Tetrameter Quatrains

"La Belle Dame Sans Merci" is divided into twelve four-line stanzas, called *quatrains*. Each of those quatrains rhymes according to an ABCB pattern. For example, take a look at the first stanza: the second line rhymes with the fourth: "loiter**ing**" and "**sing**."

That covers the rhyme, but what about the meter, or the pattern of stressed syllables? The basic meter of the poem is *iambic tetrameter*. Before you fall asleep at your computer, let us explain: "Iambic" refers to the pattern of unstressed and stressed syllables. One *iamb* is an unstressed, followed by a stressed syllable: da-DUM. "Tetrameter" tells you how many iambs you'll find per line. "Tetra" means four – so there are four iambs per line. Iambic tetrameter. Check it out in line 1:

"O **what** / can **ail** / thee, **knight** / at **arms**,

We've put the syllables that you would stress more as you read it in bold face, and we've divided up the four iambs.

But something strange happens in the fourth line of each quatrain. There are only three stressed syllables in the fourth line of each quatrain. This isn't a mistake on Keats's part. The fourth line is consistently shorter. Even if you're not used to counting stressed and unstressed syllables, you can tell just from looking at the page that the fourth line is always shorter. What's the effect of this shift in the rhythm? It's an open question. Feel free to come up with your own answers.

Furthermore, "La Belle Dame Sans Merci" is a ballad, which is an old-fashioned, folksy style of poem that typically tells a story. Ballads use simple language that would appeal to less educated people, like farmers and laborers. Ballads were primarily an oral form – people would memorize them and pass them on to their friends and family by memory, rather than from a book. Poets like Keats tried to mimic this style in their written works. Many of the Romantic

poets liked the deceptively simple form of the ballad. William Wordsworth and Samuel Taylor Coleridge famously kicked off their careers (and arguably the whole Romantic literary movement) with their collection of poems called *Lyrical Ballads*.

Speaker

"La Belle Dame Sans Merci" is in the form of a dialogue between two speakers. The first is the unnamed speaker who comes across a sick, sad knight and pesters him with questions for the first three stanzas. Stanzas 4-12 are the knight's response. There aren't any quotation marks to tip you off to the change in speaker, so you have to pay attention to notice that the "I" of stanzas 4-12 is different from the "I" of stanzas 1-3.

Having cleared that up, what kind of speaker is the unnamed person who finds the knight? Is it supposed to be the poet himself? Or is it supposed to be the reader? Or an anonymous passerby? We don't know a lot about the speaker, but we can make some guesses based on what he says in those first three stanzas. Whoever it is, he uses old-fashioned language typical of medieval romances (like "thee" and "woe-begone"). He's also very sensitive to the changes of the seasons – he doesn't just say "Hey, knight, why are you hanging out by the lake when it's so cold and dreary?" He uses a lot of rich imagery to describe the seasons. He's also very perceptive of the knight's physical and emotional state. The speaker notices that the knight is "haggard" and depressed-looking, and seems to have a fever.

The knight uses the same kind of language that the original speaker used. In fact, it's difficult to tell that it's another speaker. Usually, when poets or novelists write dialogue, they try to differentiate between the different speakers by making them sound different. But not so in "La Belle Dame Sans Merci." One possible reason for this might have to do with the ballad tradition that Keats was mimicking. Ballads are like folk songs, and they could either be sung or recited by one person, or could be divided up between different people. Having the knight and the original speaker sound the same could just be Keats's way of creating a sense of unity to the poem.

Another possible reason is that the knight is just a figment of the original speaker's imagination. After all, what happens to him is incredible, and the dream sequence at the end emphasizes the possibility of illusion. If that's the case, the knight would never have spoken, and it would have been the same speaker for the entire poem. There isn't an obvious answer to this question – critics and readers still debate the meaning of the poem today.

Sound Check

"La Belle Dame Sans Merci," like most ballads, sounds like a song. The steady rhythm of the words creates an underlying beat, and the rhyme scheme and all the alliterations make layers of sound that work like harmony in music. Even the repetition between the first and last stanza adds to the feeling that it's a song, and not a poem. You could even think of the knight's trippy dream sequence as a kind of bridge or guitar riff. We're not the only ones who think "La Belle Dame Sans Merci" would make a great song – lots of musicians have set it to music, so check out "Best of the Web" for some examples.

La Belle Dame Sans Merci
Shmoop Poetry Guide

What's Up With the Title?

"La Belle Dame Sans Merci" isn't the most obvious title in the world for an English poem, because it's not in English. It's in French and, as those of you in French 1 already figured out, it translates to "The beautiful lady without mercy." But why is the title in French? Why couldn't Keats just title it, "The beautiful lady with a heart of stone"?

Well, as you may have already guessed, the title is an *allusion* to a much earlier work of literature. It's from a medieval romance by the French poet Alain Chartier. The poem itself has many of the same elements as a medieval romance (knights, fair ladies, fairies, dream sequences…), so by titling the poem with a line from a famous romance, Keats calls up all those associations right from the beginning.

Calling Card

Too much of a good thing can kill you.

Like most of the younger generation of Romantic poets (including Lord Byron and Percy Bysshe Shelley), John Keats liked to write poems celebrating youth, sex, and beauty. "La Belle Dame Sans Merci" is no exception – except that we're not exactly wishing we were in the knight's shoes at the end of the poem. Sure, he gets the girl, but then she dumps him and leaves him out in the cold (literally). Keats seems to be pointing out to his readers, "sure, guys, sex and beauty are great, but if you obsess about them to the exclusion of everything else, you're going to die. Alone." This is advice that rock-star poets like Lord Byron could probably have used.

Tough-O-Meter

(3) Base Camp

This is not Keats's toughest poem by a long shot. On a narrative, or storytelling level, it's pretty straightforward. A knight falls in love with a beautiful fairy lady, gets ditched, and is moping about it. But the language is old-fashioned, in imitation of medieval romances, and some of the hard vocabulary words can trip up the unwary reader.

Setting

Reading "La Belle Dame Sans Merci" is like walking into a classic fairy tale. No, we don't mean the Disney kind, with happy, singing mice and twittering birds. We mean the old-school, medieval kind, with bleak landscapes, knights, fairies, and witches. The unnamed speaker at the beginning of the poem seems to have wandered into someone else's fairy tale, too. He's just out on a walk, enjoying the late autumn by a lake, when he sees a "haggard" knight who seems sick and depressed. He asks the knight what's up, and the knight launches into a long

La Belle Dame Sans Merci
Shmoop Poetry Guide

story about how he met a fairy lady in the fields somewhere. Is the knight's story all just a dream? Does the poem take place in a fairy tale, or in the real world? If it takes place partly in both, where's the border? The poem's setting seems designed to throw you off.

Themes

Theme of Love

"La Belle Dame Sans Merci" is John Keats's version of a medieval romance. It's about a knight who falls in love with a beautiful fairy lady. We immediately know that love is going to be a major theme. But where does love take us in the world of "La Belle Dame"? Not to weddings and happily ever after, that's for sure. "Love," in this poem, could be synonymous with "obsession." It's not a pretty thing.

Questions About Love

1. Was there a possible happy ending for the knight and the fairy lady, or was their romantic relationship doomed from the start?
2. In the fairy world of "La Belle Dame Sans Merci," is it possible to love someone without becoming totally obsessed? Why or why not?
3. Does the disinterested compassion that the unnamed speaker feels for the knight provide a model for a positive love in this poem?

Chew on this: Love

The relationship between the lady and the knight in "La Belle Dame Sans Merci" is doomed from the start because the two are from fundamentally different worlds.

Love fails in "La Belle Dame Sans Merci" because it is one-sided: the lady "loves" in line 19, and confesses her love in line 28, while the knight only admires her beauty.

Theme of Women and Femininity

If the knight's experience of love and sex in "La Belle Dame Sans Merci" is so negative, that we wonder what it must that say about women? Nothing good. The fairy lady in the poem enslaves the knight and then ditches him, leaving him to mope around the lake "haggard" and "pale." And this isn't the first time she's done this. According to the knight's dream, there was a whole series of "pale kings," "princes," and "warriors" whom the fairy lady ensnared before the knight came along. Of course, the story is told from the point of view of the knight, and not of the lady, so it's possible that his perception is biased or inaccurate.

La Belle Dame Sans Merci
Shmoop Poetry Guide

Questions About Women and Femininity

1. Is the speaker at the beginning male or female? How can you tell, and why would it matter?
2. Why does the fairy lady cry in the "elfin grot" (30)?
3. Why doesn't the fairy lady get to speak for herself? Why are her actions only described from the point of view of the knight?
4. Why are the lady's eyes "wild" (lines 16 and 31)? What might that suggest about her?

Chew on this: Women and Femininity

The motives of the lady in "La Belle Dame Sans Merci" are described only from the knight's point of view. Because the knight is not a reliable narrator, it is possible that the reason she weeps in her "elfin grot" (30) is that the knight has injured her in some way.

Although many feminist critics have read "La Belle Dame Sans Merci" as a pseudo-rape, the knight's ornamentation of the lady's "fragrant zone" in line 17 suggests that he is actually celebrating her femininity.

Theme of The Supernatural

"La Belle Dame Sans Merci" is part folk ballad, part romance, and part fairy tale. The lady's "wild" eyes suggest that maybe the knight isn't too far off when he calls her "a fairy's child." She appears out of nowhere, apparently lives in an "elfin grot" in the woods, and can ensnare any man she meets with her beauty, her "fairy's song," and her "language strange." Is she casting a spell over them, or are they just too easily obsessed with whatever beautiful woman is in their immediate line of sight? How much magic is there in this poem?

Questions About The Supernatural

1. How is the knight able to understand the lady's "language strange" (line 27)?
2. How does the knight know that she's a "fairy's child"? What does that mean, anyway?
3. Does the lady actually use magic on the knight? When? How can you tell?
4. Is she an evil fairy, or a misunderstood fairy?

Chew on this: The Supernatural

The lady of "La Belle Dame Sans Merci" could be read as simply a mortal woman who broke the heart of the knight. His re-telling of the story, however, casts her as supernatural in order to excuse his own weakness.

La Belle Dame Sans Merci
Shmoop Poetry Guide

Theme of Versions of Reality

The knight in "La Belle Dame Sans Merci" describes the dream he has towards the end of the poem, but the entire experience seems like a dream. Where does the dream really begin? Could the knight and his story just be a dream that the speaker is having? Are they in the real world, or in fairyland? What is real and what is fantasy in this poem?

Questions About Versions of Reality

1. "On the cold hill's side" is repeated in the fourth line of two stanzas (lines 36 and 44). Why does the knight want to emphasize where he was when he was sleeping, dreaming, and waking up?
2. Speaking of which, where is the knight when he falls asleep? In line 33, they're still in the "elfin grot," but by the time he's having the dream, he's "on the cold hill's side." When does he leave the cave? Why do you think so?
3. Could the entire story of the fairy lady just be a dream that the knight had? Explain your answer.
4. Could the knight himself be a figment of the speaker's imagination? How would that change your reading of the poem?

Chew on this: Versions of Reality

By echoing the original speaker almost word-for-word in the final stanza, the knight suggests that the sequence of events described by the poem is a self-perpetuating cycle.

The frequent repetition of images and particular words in "La Belle Dame Sans Merci" creates the impression that the poem is the dream of the unnamed speaker.

Theme of Abandonment

In a nutshell, "La Belle Dame Sans Merci" is about being abandoned by the one you love. The knight gets abandoned and left on a "cold hill's side," even though he appears to be at death's door. The beautiful fairy lady, we know from the title, is "sans merci," or merciless. She abandons him without pity, and the knight's solitude becomes the framing image of the poem.

Questions About Abandonment

1. Why does the outside world seem to reflect the inner, emotional state of the knight? When he's in love, there are lots of flowers, and after he's been abandoned, the world seems desolate. Does the world only *seem* desolate in the first three stanzas because the knight has been abandoned?
2. Why does the lady abandon the knight while he's asleep? Can't she break up with him face-to-face?
3. Has the lady abandoned all of the "pale kings," "princes," and "pale warriors" from stanza 10? Are they just her ex-lovers, or are they dead? Was she responsible for their death?

La Belle Dame Sans Merci
Shmoop Poetry Guide

Chew on this: Abandonment
The lady's abandonment of the knight is emphasized as an important theme in "La Belle Dame Sans Merci" through the repetition of the word "alone" in the first and final stanzas.

Quotes

Love Quotes

She looked at me as she did love,
And made sweet moan. (lines 19-20)

Thought: These lines are usually interpreted as a sex scene. The knight and the lady here consummate their love. At least, they're consummating *her* love. Notice that she's the subject in this sentence: she's the one doing all the "look[ing]," "lov[ing]," and "moan[ing]."

I set her on my pacing steed,
And nothing else saw all day long. (lines 21-22)

Thought: The knight is so obsessed with the beautiful lady that he spends the day gawking at her. Is this love, or obsessive lust?

And sure in language strange she said –
I love thee true. (lines 27-28)

Thought: Again, it's the lady, and not the knight, who's doing the work here. She tells him that she loves him, but he doesn't say a word.

And there I shut her wild wild eyes
With kisses four. (lines 31-32)

Thought: Finally, the knight is doing something for himself. And what is he doing? He's "shut[ting]" her eyes. Maybe the "wild[ness]" in them was starting to creep him out, or maybe he's just trying to calm her down.

And there she lulled me asleep (line 33)

Thought: Out of context, this sounds like a very loving, maternal scene – like a mother rocking a baby to sleep. Like some of the earlier passages, this line makes the knight seem passive. The lady is doing all the work, and he's just following her around and falling asleep in her "elfin grot."

**La Belle Dame Sans Merci
Shmoop Poetry Guide**

Women and Femininity Quotes

*I met a lady in the meads,
Full beautiful, a fairy's child;* (lines 13-14)

Thought: These are the lines in which the lady is first introduced. She's in the "meads," or fields when he meets her, and she's "full beautiful." The final description is a strange. Why does he call her a "fairy's *child*"? Sure, this is a fairy tale, and the lady is possibly a fairy, but why a "child"? The knight seems to infantilize her, or to treat her like a child in a condescending way, right from the get-go.

*Her hair was long, her foot was light,
And her eyes were wild.* (lines 15-16)

Thought: This description breaks the fairy lady into her component parts, telling us about her "hair," her "foot," and her "eyes." It's like the knight is dissecting her with this description.

*I made a garland for her head,
And bracelets too, and fragrant zone;* (lines 17-18)

Thought: By placing the "garland" of flowers on the lady's head, the knight is symbolically crowning her as queen of his heart. But the "fragrant zone," or flower belt, that he puts around her waist suggests that she's queen of other parts, too.

*She took me to her elfin grot,
And there she wept, and sigh'd full sore,* (lines 29-30)

Thought: After riding around on the knight's horse all day, the fairy lady invites the knight back to her "elfin grot," or cave. But why does she start crying and sighing? Is it because she regrets having sex with the knight? Or because she's sorry for what she's going to do to him? If she's feeling remorse, why does she abandon him, anyway? This is one of the most ambiguous lines of the poem.

*And there I shut her wild wild eyes
With kisses four.* (lines 31-32)

Thought: Again, the fairy lady's eyes are described as "wild," and this time, the knight calls attention to this wildness through repetition. One of the fairy lady's defining characteristics is her "wild wild eyes," so it's important that the knight tries to neutralize them by "shut[ting]" them.

La Belle Dame Sans Merci
Shmoop Poetry Guide

And there she lulled me asleep (line 33)

Thought: The sweet, almost maternal feel of this line conflicts with the anxiety the reader feels about what the fairy lady is going to do to the knight once he's asleep.

The Supernatural Quotes

[…] A fairy's child (line 14)

Thought: This is the first hint that the lady is in some way associated with the supernatural. This line doesn't make it clear whether the lady *is* a fairy, or whether she's just so beautiful and mysterious that she *seems* like "a fairy's child."

For sidelong would she bend, and sing
A fairy's song (lines 23-24)

Thought: Again, it's possible to read this as romantic *hyperbole*, or overstatement. Is she really singing a magical, "fairy's song," or is her voice so sweet to the enraptured knight that it sounds magical to him?

She found me roots of relish sweet,
And honey wild, and manna dew, (lines 25-26)

Thought: Giving the knight "manna" makes the lady seem almost divine. "[M]anna" is the heavenly food that the Israelites ate after they escaped from slavery in Egypt, according to the Jewish scriptures. But it's possible that the knight's perception of the honey, roots, and water she gave him is colored by his obsession with her. Maybe it was just ordinary spring water, but he was so in love, that it seemed like heavenly "manna dew" to him.

And sure in language strange she said – (line 27)

Thought: The lady speaks in a strange language. Is it actually a different language, or does she just have an accent? Or is she speaking a different version of English (perhaps a more everyday, common language) from what the upper-class knight is used to? It's unclear.

She took me to her elfin grot (line 29)

Thought: The lady takes the knight to her "elfin," or elfish cave. Was it filled with obvious signs of magic or witchcraft? How does he know that it's "elfin," and not just a cave where this lady lives? We don't get any of the details, so it's hard to tell.

La Belle Dame Sans Merci
Shmoop Poetry Guide

Versions of Reality Quotes

O what can ail thee, knight at arms,
Alone and palely loitering (lines 1-2)

Thought: The knight seems almost ghost-like in these first lines. The speaker finds him all "alone" and "loitering" near a lake. He's pale like a ghost, and the "loitering" seems like a ghost that haunts the place where he died.

I see a lily on thy brow
With anguish moist and fever dew (lines 9-10)

Thought: The speaker can tell that the knight has a fever. High fevers can cause hallucinations or visions. Is it possible that the knight is just a sick man who had a feverish dream about a fairy lady who seduced him and then ditched him?

And nothing else saw all day long (line 22)

Thought: The knight is so obsessed with the beautiful lady that he doesn't even *see* anything else. He's blind to the rest of the world.

And there I dream'd – Ah! woe betide!
The latest dream I ever dream'd
On the cold hill's side. (lines 34-36)

Thought: The word "dream" gets repeated three times in these lines. Why is that? Does the knight want to emphasize that it was, in fact, a dream, and not a real series of ghosts that he saw? The knight's dream was so horrific that he interrupts himself with that dash and interjection – "Ah! woe betide!"

I saw pale kings, and princes too,
Pale warriors, death pale were they all; (lines 37-38)

Thought: More repetition in these lines. This time, it's the word "pale" as the knight describes his dream.

They cried – "La belle dame sans merci
Hath thee in thrall!" (lines 39-40)

Thought: These lines have to be important, because they contain the title of the poem. They're also the only lines that are set off by quotation marks, to show that they weren't spoken by either the knight or the original speaker. These lines are the warning that the ghostly "pale

La Belle Dame Sans Merci
Shmoop Poetry Guide

kings," "princes," and "warriors" cry out to the knight in his dream.

Abandonment Quotes

O what can ail thee, knight at arms,
Alone and palely loitering? (lines 1-2)

Thought: The opening image of the poem is the knight looking "pale" and "ail[ing]" while hanging out "alone." Clearly, this guy doesn't want to be alone. Even that opening syllable, "O" suggests emptiness (it looks like a zero).

And no birds sing. (line 4)

Thought: Even the birds have abandoned the knight. Poor guy.

O what can ail thee, knight at arms,
So haggard and so woe-begone? (lines 5-6)

Thought: As thought the knight needs to be reminded that he's miserable, the opening speaker repeats the same question again in the second stanza, this time commenting on the knight's "haggard" looks.

And on thy cheeks a fading rose
Fast withereth too. (lines 11-12)

Thought: The "fading rose" on the knight's "cheeks" suggests his sickly paleness (his cheeks are no longer "rosy"), but the "fading rose" also suggests a failed love affair, since roses so often represent love.

And I awoke and found me here
On the cold hill's side (lines 43-44)

Thought: After the knight wakes up from his nightmare about the "pale kings," he finds himself, quite literally, out in the cold.

And this is why I sojourn here,
Alone and palely loitering, (lines 45-46)

Thought: The knight thinks that his crazy story about the beautiful lady and her "elfin grot" is an adequate answer to the opening speaker's question about what "ails" him. Of course, the story is so ambiguous that it's not much of an answer at all.

La Belle Dame Sans Merci
Shmoop Poetry Guide

Study Questions

1. Why do you think that the fairy lady cries in her cave (line 30)?
2. Could the knight's entire experience just have been a dream? Would that matter?
3. Why is the knight able to understand the fairy lady's "language strange" (line 27)?
4. Who is the unnamed speaker who comes across the knight at the beginning of the poem? The poet, John Keats? The reader? Someone else?
5. Why does the last stanza echo the first? What is the effect of that?

Did You Know?

Trivia

- Unlike the other major Romantic poets, John Keats came from an obscure, lower-middle-class background. He was the son of a stables manager in East London (the rich people lived in the West End). He was mostly self-taught – his formal education ended when his parents died. He was only fourteen when he left school to learn to be an apothecary (a pharmacist). When he started writing poetry, most critics dismissed him as an upstart. After all, they argued, how can anyone who isn't fluent in Latin and Ancient Greek write good poetry? (Source)
- John Keats's mother died of tuberculosis. Some modern doctors think that John Keats contracted the infection from her, and that it was dormant for many years before he got sick in 1819. But most people believe that he caught it from his brother, Tom, whom he took care of in 1818. (Source)
- Like the knight in "La Belle Dame Sans Merci," Keats suffered from some serious love problems. But his girl didn't leave him for dead "on a cold hill's side." Keats was engaged to be married to Fanny Brawne, but they were kept apart first because of Keats's financial problems, and then because of his terminal illness. Their relationship was pretty rocky from the beginning, but she remained loyal to him through the end of his life. (Source)

Steaminess Rating

La Belle Dame Sans Merci
Shmoop Poetry Guide

PG-13
There is definitely some fairy lady/knight-at-arms action going on in stanza 5, but it's not very explicit, so we're giving it a PG-13.

Allusions and Cultural References

Literature, Philosophy, and Mythology

- "La Belle Dame Sans Merci" (Title and line 39): The title of the poem is taken from a medieval French courtly romance by Alain Chartier.
- "Pale warriors, death pale were they all…" (line 38): this could be a reference to the fourth horseman of the Apocalypse described in the Book of Revelation in the Christian Bible – the fourth horseman is Death, and he's described repeatedly as riding a "pale horse."

Best of the Web

Websites

The Victorian Web
http://www.victorianweb.org/previctorian/keats/keatsov.html
This is a handy website for anyone studying the 19th century (not just the Victorian Period, which is only from 1837-1901). This is the link to the John Keats portion of the site, which has a biography and timeline of his short life, as well as other great resources.

The British Library's Online Gallery
http://www.bl.uk/onlinegallery/features/keats/keats.html
The British Library in London is one of the largest, most important collections in the world. Even if you can't visit in person, their website provides some useful information about the writers whose manuscripts are kept there. This is a link to a British Library page about John Keats.

Video

Movie Trailer for "La Belle Dame Sans Merci"
http://www.youtube.com/watch?v=Vb5477wW9QU
In this video, actors act out the poem.

Ray Archer Trio's "La Belle Dame Sans Merci"
http://www.youtube.com/watch?v=YOZrOs2dALg
A music video of "La Belle Dame Sans Merci" by the Ray Archer Trio.

Penda's Fen "La Belle Dame Sans Merci"

La Belle Dame Sans Merci
Shmoop Poetry Guide

http://www.youtube.com/watch?v=b8lMp1Nl2Ow
This is a video of a rendition of Keats's poem set to music by the group Penda's Fen.

Audio
"La Belle Dame Sans Merci" Out Loud
http://www.youtube.com/watch?v=NdTp1d8SZVI
This is a reading of "La Belle Dame Sans Merci" accompanied by some of the paintings inspired by the poem.

Images
J.W. Waterhouse Painting
http://www.uweb.ucsb.edu/%7Ekfopma/La-Belle-Dame-Sans-Merci-Print-C10078774.jpeg
One of the paintings by John William Waterhouse inspired by Keats's poem.

Sir Frank Dicksee's Painting
http://www.cwrl.utexas.edu/%7Ebump/E392M/cp/WindAmongtheReeds/DikseeBelleDameSansMerci.jpg
This is a link to the painting of "La Belle Dame Sans Merci" by Sir Frank Dicksee.

A Pen and Ink Sketch
http://www.gutenberg.org/files/19105/19105-h/images/440.png
This image is from a magazine called *Punch* in 1920 – the picture is titled, "La Belle Dame Sans Merci."

Pen and Ink Portrait of John Keats
http://www.bl.uk/onlinegallery/features/keats/images/keats-portrait.jpg
This simple sketch of the poet is housed at the British Library in London.

Miniature of John Keats
http://www.keats-shelley-house.org/img/photos/keats_him.jpg
This miniature portrait of John Keats is by Joseph Severn, and is housed at the Keats-Shelley Museum.

Photo of John Keats's Gravestone
http://englishhistory.net/keats/grave-small.jpg
This is a modern photograph of Keats's grave in the Protestant cemetery in Rome, Italy.

Historical Documents
Excerpts from John Keats's Letters
http://academic.brooklyn.cuny.edu/english/melani/cs6/keatsltr.html
John Keats wrote some sweet love letters to his fiancée, Fanny Brawne, as well as some regular, newsy letters to his friends and family. Click here to see excerpts from some of his letters.

La Belle Dame Sans Merci
Shmoop Poetry Guide

Books

Charles Armitage Brown's *The Life of John Keats*
http://englishhistory.net/keats/brownkeats.html
Charles Brown was one of John Keats's closest friends, and he wrote an early biography of Keats. (It was completed twenty years after Keats's death.) This website describes the biography and has some excerpts, or you can check a copy out of your local library for the whole thing.

Sidney Colvin's Biography of John Keats
http://englishhistory.net/keats/colvinkeats.html
This is a link to the complete text of Sidney Colvin's 1917 biography of John Keats.

Collection of John Keats's Letters
http://www.hup.harvard.edu/catalog/KEASEL.html
This is an edited collection of John Keats's letters, so if the excerpts aren't enough for you, you can check this book out of your library.

Movies and TV

"La Belle Dame Sans Merci"
http://www.imdb.com/title/tt0455346/
A 2005 movie based on the poem by John Keats.

Shmoop's Poetry Primer

How to Read Poem

There's really only one reason that poetry has gotten a reputation for being so darned "difficult": it demands your full attention and won't settle for less. Unlike a novel, where you can drift in and out and still follow the plot, poems are generally shorter and more intense, with less of a conventional story to follow. If you don't make room for the *experience*, you probably won't have one.

But the rewards can be high. To make an analogy with rock and roll, it's the difference between a two and a half minute pop song with a hook that you get sick of after the third listen, and a slow-building tour de force that sounds fresh and different every time you hear it. Once you've gotten a taste of the really rich stuff, you just want to listen to it over and over again and figure out: how'd they do that?

Aside from its demands on your attention, there's nothing too tricky about reading a poem. Like anything, it's a matter of practice. But in case you haven't read much (or any) poetry before, we've put together a short list of tips that will make it a whole lot more enjoyable.

- **Follow Your Ears.** It's okay to ask, "What does it mean?" when reading a poem. But it's even better to ask, "How does it sound?" If all else fails, treat it like a song. Even if you

La Belle Dame Sans Merci
Shmoop Poetry Guide

can't understand a single thing about a poem's "subject" or "theme," you can always say something – anything – about the sound of the words. Does the poem move fast or slow? Does it sound awkward in sections or does it have an even flow? Do certain words stick out more than others? Trust your inner ear: if the poem sounds strange, it doesn't mean you're reading it wrong. In fact, you probably just discovered one of the poem's secret tricks! If you get stuck at any point, just look for Shmoop's "Sound Check" section. We'll help you listen!

- **Read It Aloud.** OK, we're not saying you have to shout it from the rooftops. If you're embarrassed and want to lock yourself in the attic and read the poem in the faintest whisper possible, go ahead. Do whatever it takes, because reading even part of poem aloud can totally change your perspective on how it works.
- **Become an Archaeologist.** When you've drunk in the poem enough times, experiencing the sound and images found there, it is sometimes fun to switch gears and to become an archaeologist (you know -- someone who digs up the past and uncovers layers of history). Treat the poem like a room you have just entered. Perhaps it's a strange room that you've never seen before, filled with objects or people that you don't really recognize. Maybe you feel a bit like Alice in Wonderland. Assume your role as an archaeologist and take some measurements. What's the weather like? Are there people there? What kind of objects do you find? Are there more verbs than adjectives? Do you detect a rhythm? Can you hear music? Is there furniture? Are there portraits of past poets on the walls? Are there traces of other poems or historical references to be found? Check out Shmoop's "Setting," "Symbols, Imagery, Wordplay," and "Speaker" sections to help you get started.
- **Don't Skim.** Unlike the newspaper or a textbook, the point of poetry isn't to cram information into your brain. We can't repeat it enough: poetry is an experience. If you don't have the patience to get through a long poem, no worries, just start with a really short poem. Understanding poetry is like getting a suntan: you have to let it sink in. When you glance at Shmoop's "Detailed Summary," you'll see just how loaded each line of poetry can be.
- **Memorize!** "Memorize" is such a scary word, isn't it? It reminds us of multiplication tables. Maybe we should have said: "Tuck the poem into your snuggly memory-space." Or maybe not. At any rate, don't tax yourself: if you memorize one or two lines of a poem, or even just a single cool-sounding phrase, it will start to work on you in ways you didn't know possible. You'll be walking through the mall one day, and all of a sudden, you'll shout, "I get it!" Just not too loud, or you'll get mall security on your case.
- **Be Patient.** You can't really understand a poem that you've only read once. You just can't. So if you don't get it, set the poem aside and come back to it later. And by "later" we mean days, months, or even years. Don't rush it. It's a much bigger accomplishment to actually *enjoy* a poem than it is to be able to explain every line of it. Treat the first reading as an investment – your effort might not pay off until well into the future, but when it does, it will totally be worth it. Trust us.
- **Read in Crazy Places.** Just like music, the experience of poetry changes depending on your mood and the environment. Read in as many different places as possible: at the beach, on a mountain, in the subway. Sometimes all it takes is a change of scenery for a poem to really come alive.
- **Think Like a Poet.** Here's a fun exercise. Go through the poem one line at a time, covering up the next line with your hand so you can't see it. Put yourself in the poet's

shoes: If I had to write a line to come after this line, what would I put? If you start to think like this, you'll be able to appreciate all the different choices that go into making a poem. It can also be pretty humbling – at least we think so. Shmoop's "Calling Card" section will help you become acquainted with a poet's particular, unique style. Soon, you'll be able to decipher a T.S. Elliot poem from a Wallace Stevens poem, sight unseen. Everyone will be so jealous.

- **"Look Who's Talking."** Ask the most basic questions possible of the poem. Two of the most important are: "Who's talking?" and "Who are they talking to?" If it's a Shakespeare sonnet, don't just assume that the speaker is Shakespeare. The speaker of every poem is kind of fictional creation, and so is the audience. Ask yourself: what would it be like to meet this person? What would they look like? What's their "deal," anyway? Shmoop will help you get to know a poem's speaker through the "Speaker" section found in each study guide.
- And, most importantly, **Never Be Intimidated.** Regardless of what your experience with poetry in the classroom has been, no poet wants to make his or her audience feel stupid. It's just not good business, if you know what we mean. Sure, there might be tricky parts, but it's not like you're trying to unlock the secrets of the universe. Heck, if you want to ignore the "meaning" entirely, then go ahead. Why not? If you're still feeling a little timid, let Shmoop's "Why Should I Care" section help you realize just how much you have to bring to the poetry table.

Poetry is about freedom and exposing yourself to new things. In fact, if you find yourself stuck in a poem, just remember that the poet, 9 times out of 10, was a bit of a rebel and was trying to make his friends look at life in a completely different way. Find your inner rebel too. There isn't a single poem out there that's "too difficult" to try out – right now, today. So hop to it. As you'll discover here at Shmoop, there's plenty to choose from.

Sources:

http://allpoetry.com/column/2339540
http://academic.reed.edu/writing/paper_help/figurative_language.html
http://web.uvic.ca/wguide/Pages/LiteraryTermsTOC.html#RhetLang
http://www.tnellen.com/cybereng/lit_terms/allegory.html

What is Poetry?

What is poetry? At the most basic level, poetry is an *experience* produced by two elements of language: "sense" and "sound." The "sense" of a word is its meaning. The word "cat" refers to a small, furry animal with whiskers, a long tail, and, if you're unlucky, a knack for scratching up all your new furniture. We can all agree that's what "cat" means. But "cat" also has a particular sound when you say it, and this sound is different from similar words for "cat" in other languages.

La Belle Dame Sans Merci
Shmoop Poetry Guide

Most of the things that you hear, say, or read in your daily life (including the words you are reading right now) put more emphasis on meaning than on sound. Not so with poetry. Have you ever repeated a word so many times that it started to sound strange and foreign? No? Try saying that word "cat" twenty times in a row. "Cat, cat, cat, cat, cat, cat . . ." Kind of weird, right? Well, guess what: you just made poetry out of a single word – that is, you turned the word into an experience that is as much about sound as it is about sense. Congratulations, poet!

Or let's imagine that you type the words "blue" and "ocean" on a page all by their lonesome selves. These two little words are quite ordinary and pop up in conversations all the time. However, when we see them isolated, all alone on a page, they might just take on a whole new meaning. Maybe "blue ocean" looks like a little strand of islands in a big sea of white space, and maybe we start to think about just how big the ocean is. Or you could reverse the order and type the words as "ocean blue," which would bring up a slightly different set of connotations, such as everyone's favorite grade-school rhyme: "In 1492 Columbus sailed the ocean blue."

Poetry is also visual, and so it's a good idea to pay attention to how the words are assembled on the page. Our imaginations are often stirred by a poem's visual presentation. Just like a person, poems can send all kinds of signals with their physical appearance. Some are like a slick businessman in a suit or a woman in an evening gown. Their lines are all regularized and divided neatly into even stanzas. Others are like a person at a rock concert who is dressed in tattered jeans, a ragged t-shirt, and a Mohawk, and who has tattoos and piercings all over their body! And some poems, well, some poems look like a baked potato that exploded in your microwave. It's always a good idea to ask yourself how the appearance of words on the page interacts with the meaning of those words. If the poem is about war, maybe it looks like a battle is going on, and the words are fighting for space. If the poem is about love, maybe the lines are spaced to appear as though they are dancing with one another. Often the appearance and meaning will be in total contrast, which is just as interesting.

OK, that's a very broad idea of what poetry is. Let's narrow it down a bit. When most people talk about poetry, they are talking about a particular kind of literature that is broken up into lines, or *verses*. In fact, for most of history, works divided into verse were considered more "literary" than works in prose. Even those long stories called "epics," like Homer's *The Odyssey* and Virgil's *Aeneid*, are actually poems.

Now, you're thinking: "Wait a minute, I thought verses belong to songs and music." Exactly. The very first poets – from Biblical times and even before – set their poems to music, and it's still acceptable to refer to a poem as a "song." For example, the most famous work by the American poet Walt Whitman is titled, "Song of Myself." Because of their shared emphasis on sound, poetry and music have always been like blood brothers.

The last thing to say about poetry is that it doesn't like to be pinned down. That's why there's no single definition that fits all of the things that we would call "poems." Just when you think you have poetry cornered, and you're ready to define it as literature broken into lines, it breaks free and shouts, "Aha! You forgot about the *prose poem*, which doesn't have any verses!" Drats! Fortunately, we get the last laugh, because we can enjoy and recognize poems even without a perfect definition of what poetry is.

La Belle Dame Sans Merci
Shmoop Poetry Guide

Sources:

http://allpoetry.com/column/2339540
http://academic.reed.edu/writing/paper_help/figurative_language.html
http://web.uvic.ca/wguide/Pages/LiteraryTermsTOC.html#RhetLang
http://www.tnellen.com/cybereng/lit_terms/allegory.html

Poetry Glossary

Allegory: An allegory is a kind of extended metaphor (a metaphor that weaves throughout the poem) in which objects, persons, and actions stand for another meaning.

Alliteration: Alliteration happens when words that begin with the same sound are placed close to one another. For example, "the **s**illy **s**nake **s**ilently **s**linked by" is a form of alliteration. Try saying that ten times fast.

Allusion: An allusion happens when a speaker or character makes a brief and casual reference to a famous historical or literary figure or event.

Anaphora: Anaphora involves the repetition of the same word or group of words at the beginning of successive clauses or sections. Think of an annoying kid on a road trip: "Are we there yet? / Are we going to stop soon? / Are we having lunch soon?". Not a poem we'd like to read in its entirety, but the repetition of the word "are" is anaphora.

Anthologize: To put in a poetry anthology, usually for teaching purposes, so that students have a broad selection of works to choose from. Usually, the word will come up in a context like this: "That's one of her most famous poems. I've seen it anthologized a lot." An anthology is a book that has samples of the work of a lot of different writers. It's like a plate of appetizers so you can try out a bunch of stuff. You can also find anthologies for different periods, like Romantic, Modern, and Postmodern. The Norton, Columbia, and Best American anthologies are three of the most famous.

Apostrophe: Apostrophe is when an idea, person, object, or absent being is addressed as if it or they were present, alive, and kicking. John Donne uses apostrophe when he writes this: "Death be not proud, though some have called thee / Mighty and dreadful."

Avant Garde: You'll hear this word used to describe some of the craziest, most far-out, experimental poets. It was originally a French expression that refers to the soldiers who go explore a territory before the main army comes in. Avant garde artists are often people who break through boundaries and do what's never been done before. Then again, sometimes there's a good reason why something has been done before…

Ballad: A ballad is a song: think boy bands and chest-thumping emotion. But in poetry, a ballad

La Belle Dame Sans Merci
Shmoop Poetry Guide

is ancient form of storytelling. In the (very) old days, common people didn't get their stories from books – they were sung as musical poems. Because they are meant to convey information, ballads usually have a simple rhythm and a consistent rhyme scheme. They often tell the story of everyday heroes, and some poets, like Bob Dylan, continue to set them to music.

Blank Verse: Thanks to Shakespeare and others, blank verse is one of the most common forms of English poetry. It's verse that has no rhyme scheme but has a regular meter. Usually this meter is iambic pentameter (check out our definition below). Why is blank verse so common in English? Well, a lot of people think we speak in it in our everyday conversations. Kind of like we just did: "a LOT of PEO-ple THINK we SPEAK in IT." That could be a blank verse line.

Cadence: Cadence refers to the rhythmic or musical elements of a poem. You can think of it as the thing that makes poetry sound like poetry. Whereas "meter" refers to the regular elements of rhythm – the beats or accents – "cadence" refers to the momentary variations in rhythm, like when a line speeds up or slows down. Poets often repeat or contrast certain cadences to create a more interesting sound than normal prose.

Caesura: A fancy word for a pause that occurs in the middle of a line of verse. Use this if want to sound smart, but we think "pause" is just fine. You can create pauses in a lot of ways, but the most obvious is to use punctuation like a period, comma, or semicolon. Note that a pause at the end of a line is not a caesura.

Chiasmus: Chiasmus consists of two parallel phrases in which corresponding words or phrases are placed in the opposite order: "Fair is foul, foul is fair."

Cliché: Clichés are phrases or expressions that are used so much in everyday life, that people roll their eyes when they hear them. For example, "dead as a doornail" is a cliché. In good poetry, clichés are never used with a straight face, so if you see one, consider why the speaker might be using it.

Concrete Poetry: Concrete poetry conveys meaning by how it looks on the page. It's not a super-accurate term, and it can refer to a lot of different kinds of poems. One classic example is poems that look like they thing they describe. The French poet Guillaume Apollinaire wrote a poem about Paris in the shape of the Eiffel tower.

Connotation: The suggestive meaning of a word – the associations it brings up. The reason it's not polite to call a mentally-handicapped person "retarded" is that the word has a *negative* connotation. Connotations depend a lot on the culture and experience of the person reading the word. For some people, the word "liberal" has a positive connotation. For others, it's negative. Think of connotation as the murky haze hanging around the literal meaning of a word. Trying to figure out connotations of words can be one of the most confusing and fascinating aspects of reading poetry.

Contradiction: Two statements that don't seem to agree with each other. "I get sober when I drink alcohol" is a contradiction. Some contradictions, like "paradox" (see our definition below), are only apparent, and they become true when you think about them in a certain way.

La Belle Dame Sans Merci
Shmoop Poetry Guide

Denotation: The literal, straightforward meaning of a word. It's "dictionary definition." The word "cat" denotes an animal with four legs and a habit of coughing up furballs.

Dramatic Monologue: You can think of a dramatic monologue in poetry as a speech taken from a play that was never written. Okay, maybe that's confusing. It's a poem written in the voice of a fictional character and delivered to a fictional listener, instead of in the voice of a poet to his or her readers. The British poet Robert Browning is one of the most famous writers of dramatic monologues. They are "dramatic" because they can be acted out, just like a play, and they are monologues because they consist of just one person speaking to another person, just as a "dialogue" consists of two people speaking. (The prefix "mono" means "one," whereas "di" means "two").

Elegy: An elegy is a poem about a dead person or thing. Whenever you see a poem with the title, "In Memory of . . .", for example, you're talking about an elegy. Kind of like that two-line poem you wrote for your pet rabbit Bubbles when you were five years old. Poor, poor Bubbles.

Ellipsis: You see ellipses all the time, usually in the form of "…". An ellipsis involves leaving out or suppressing words. It's like . . . well, you get the idea.

Enjambment: When a phrase carries over a line-break without a major pause. In French, the word means, "straddling," which we think is a perfect way to envision an enjambed line. Here's an example of enjambment from a poem by Joyce Kilmer: 'I think that I shall never see / A poem as lovely as a tree." The sentence continues right over the break with only a slight pause.

Extended metaphor: A central metaphor that acts like an "umbrella" to connect other metaphors or comparisons within it. It can span several lines or an entire poem. When one of Shakespeare's characters delivers an entire speech about how all the world is a stage and people are just actors, that's extended metaphor, with the idea of "theater" being the umbrella connecting everything.

Foot: The most basic unit of a poem's meter, a foot is a combination of long and short syllables. There are all kinds of different feet, such as "LONG-short" and "short-short-LONG." The first three words of the famous holiday poem, "'Twas the Night before Christmas," are one metrical foot (short-short-LONG). By far the most important foot to know is the iamb: short-LONG. An iamb is like one heartbeat: ba-DUM.

Free Verse: "Free bird! Play free bird!" Oops, we meant "Free verse! Define free verse!" Free verse is a poetic style that lacks a regular meter or rhyme scheme. This may sound like free verse has no style at all, but usually there is some recognizable consistency to the writer's use of rhythm. Walt Whitman was one of the pioneers of free verse, and nobody ever had trouble identifying a Whitman poem.

Haiku: A poetic form invented by the Japanese. In English, the haiku has three sections with five syllables, seven syllables, and five syllables respectively. They often describe natural imagery and include a word that reveals the season in which the poem is set. Aside from its three sections, the haiku also traditionally features a sharp contrast between two ideas or

**La Belle Dame Sans Merci
Shmoop Poetry Guide**

images.

Heroic Couplet: Heroic couplets are rhyming pairs of verse in iambic pentameter. What on earth did this "couplets" do to become "heroic"? Did they pull a cat out of a tree or save an old lady from a burning building? In fact, no. They are called "heroic" because in the old days of English poetry they were used to talk about the trials and adventures of heroes. Although heroic couplets totally ruled the poetry scene for a long time, especially in the 17th and 18th centuries, nowadays they can sound kind of old-fashioned.

Hyperbole: A hyperbole is a gross exaggeration. For example, "tons of money" is a hyperbole.

Iambic Pentameter: Here it is, folks. Probably the single most useful technical term in poetry. Let's break it down: an "iamb" is an unaccented syllable followed by an accented one. "Penta" means "five," and "meter" refers to a regular rhythmic pattern. So "iambic pentameter" is a kind of *rhythmic pattern* that consist of *five iambs* per line. It's the most common rhythm in English poetry and sounds like five heartbeats: ba-DUM, ba-DUM, ba-DUM, ba-DUM, ba-DUM. Let's try it out on the first line of Shakespeare's *Romeo and Juliet*: "In fair Verona, where we lay our scene." Every second syllable is accented, so this is classic iambic pentameter.

Imagery: Imagery is intense, descriptive language in a poem that helps to trigger our senses and our memories when we read it.

Irony: Irony involves saying one thing while really meaning another, contradictory thing.

Metaphor: A metaphor happens when one thing is described as being another thing. "You're a toad!" is a metaphor – although not a very nice one. And metaphor is different from simile because it leaves out the words "like" or "as." For example, a simile would be, "You're *like* a toad."

Metonymy: Metonymy happens when some attribute of what is being described is used to indicate some other attribute. When talking about the power of a king, for example, one may instead say "the crown"-- that is, the physical attribute that is usually identified with royalty and power.

Ode: A poem written in praise or celebration of a person, thing, or event. Odes have been written about everything from famous battles and lofty emotions to family pets and household appliances. What would you write an ode about?

Onomatopoeia: Besides being a really fun word to say aloud, onomatopoeia refers either to words that resemble in sound what they represent. For example, do you hear the hissing noise when you say the word "hiss" aloud? And the old Batman television show *loved* onomatopoeia: "Bam! Pow! Kaplow!"

Oxymoron: An oxymoron is the combination of two terms ordinarily seen as opposites. For example, "terribly good" is an oxymoron.

La Belle Dame Sans Merci
Shmoop Poetry Guide

Paradox: A statement that contradicts itself and nonetheless seems true. It's a paradox when John Donne writes, "Death, thou shalt die," because he's using "death" in two different senses. A more everyday example might be, "Nobody goes to the restaurant because it's too crowded."

Parallelism: Parallelism happens a lot in poetry. It is the similarity of structure in a pair or series of related words, phrases, or clauses. Julius Caesar's famous words, "I came, I saw, I conquered," are an example of parallelism. Each clause begins with "I" and ends with a verb.

Pastoral: A poem about nature or simple, country life. If the poem you're reading features babbling brooks, gently swaying trees, hidden valleys, rustic haystacks, and sweetly singing maidens, you're probably dealing with a pastoral. The oldest English pastoral poems were written about the English countryside, but there are plenty of pastorals about the American landscape, too.

Personification: Personification involves giving human traits (qualities, feelings, action, or characteristics) to non-living objects (things, colors, qualities, or ideas).

Pun: A pun is a play on words. Puns show us the multiple meanings of a word by replacing that word with another that is similar in sound but has a very different meaning. For example, "when Shmoop went trick-or-treating in a Batman costume, he got lots of snickers." Hehe.

Quatrain: A stanza with four lines. Quatrains are the most common stanza form.

Refrain: A refrain is a regularly recurring phrase or verse especially at the end of each stanza or division of a poem or song. For example in T.S. Eliot's *Love Song for J. Alfred Prufrock*, the line, "in the room the women come and go / Talking of Michelangelo" is a refrain.

Rhetorical Question: Rhetorical questions involve asking a question for a purpose other than obtaining the information requested. For example, when we ask, "Shmoop, are you nuts?", we are mainly expressing our belief that Shmoop is crazy. In this case, we don't really expect Shmoop to tell us whether or not they are nuts.

Rhyming Couplet: A rhyming couplet is a pair of verses that rhyme. It's the simplest and most common rhyme scheme, but it can have more complicated variations (see "Heroic Couplet" for one example).

Simile: Similes compare one thing directly to another. For example, "My love is like a burning flame" is a simile. You can quickly identify similes when you see the words "like" or "as" used, as in "x is like y." Similes are different from metaphors – for example, a metaphor would refer to "the burning flame of my love."

Slam: A form of contemporary poetry that is meant to be performed at informal competitions rather than read. Slam readings are often very political in nature and draw heavily from the rhythms and energy of hip-hop music.

La Belle Dame Sans Merci
Shmoop Poetry Guide

Slant Rhyme: A rhyme that isn't quite a rhyme. The words "dear" and "door" form a slant rhyme. The words sound similar, but they aren't close enough to make a full rhyme.

Sonnet: A well-known poetic form. Two of the most famous examples are the sonnets of William Shakespeare and John Donne. A traditional sonnet has fourteen lines in iambic pentameter and a regular rhyme scheme. Sonnets also feature a "turn" somewhere in the middle, where the poem takes a new direction or changes its argument in some way. This change can be subtle or really obvious. Although we English-speaking folks would love to take credit fort this amazing form, it was actually developed by the Italians and didn't arrive in England until the 16th century.

Speaker: The speaker is the voice *behind* the poem – the person we imagine to be speaking. It's important to note that the speaker is *not* the poet. Even if the poem is biographical, you should treat the speaker as a fictional creation, because the writer is choosing what to say about himself. Besides, even poets don't speak in poetry in their everyday lives – although it would be cool if they did.

Stanza: A division within a poem where a group of lines are formed into a unit. The word "stanza" comes from the Italian word for "room." Just like a room, a poetic stanza is set apart on a page by four "walls" of blank, white space.

Symbol: Generally speaking, a symbol is a sign representing something other than itself.

Synecdoche: In synecdoche a part of something represents the whole. For example: "One does not live by bread alone." The statement assumes that bread is representative of all categories of food.

Syntax: In technical terms, syntax is the study of how to put sentences together. In poetry, "syntax" refers to the way words and phrases relate to each other. Some poems have a syntax similar to everyday prose of spoken English (like the sentences you're reading right now). Other poems have a crazier syntax, where it's hard to see how things fit together at all. It can refer to the order of words in a sentence, like Yoda's wild syntax from the *Star Wars* movies: "A very important concept in poetry, syntax is!" Or, more figuratively, it can refer to the organization of ideas or topics in a poem: "Why did the poet go from talking about his mother to a description of an ostrich?"

Understatement: An understatement seeks to express a thought or impression by underemphasizing the extent to which a statement may be true. Understatement is the opposite of hyperbole and is frequently used for its comedic value in articles, speeches, etc. when issues of great importance are being discussed. Ex: "There's just one, tiny, little problem with that plan – it'll get us all killed!"

Sources:

http://allpoetry.com/column/2339540
http://academic.reed.edu/writing/paper_help/figurative_language.html

http://web.uvic.ca/wguide/Pages/LiteraryTermsTOC.html#RhetLang
http://www.tnellen.com/cybereng/lit_terms/allegory.html

Printed in Great Britain
by Amazon.co.uk, Ltd.,
Marston Gate.